What You DON'T KNOW About

DANGEROUS PLACES

Find other fascinating facts in:

ANIMALS
MYSTERIOUS PLACES

What You DON'T KNOW About

DANGEROUS PLACES

by Ryder Windham

AN
APPLE
PAPERBACK

SCHOLASTIC INC.

New York   Toronto   London   Auckland   Sydney
Mexico City   New Delhi   Hong Kong   Buenos Aires

For Allan Kausch

Acknowledgments: Special thanks to my editors, Erin Soderberg and David Levithan, and designer Joyce White.

ISBN 0-439-22541-8

12 11 10 9 8 7 6 5 4 3 2 1   2 3 4 5 6 7/0

Printed in the U.S.A.   40
First Scholastic printing, March 2002

CONTENTS

INTRODUCTION

Wars may ravage entire countries, but some places are life-threatening even during times of peace. What makes such a place so dangerous? There may be many different factors, including geographic conditions, harsh weather, wild animals, and a location that is either far from civilization or inhabited by many people.

Indeed, the presence of people usually determines or affects our perception of the danger. Unless lives are at risk, news services might not even mention a raging snowstorm or an earthquake in a remote, unpopulated area. Our planet is surrounded by space, but it seems the only time we hear about the hazards of space is when astronauts are in trouble or a satellite is falling out of orbit.

Are you content to remain on firm ground

in familiar surroundings, or do you feel compelled to explore dangerous places? Maybe you're not sure? This book might help you find the answer.

The Amazon

LOCATION: South America

DESCRIPTION: An immense ecosystem that includes the largest tropical rain forest and second longest river on earth.

Could you survive in a dense jungle? If your answer is "I don't know," then chances are you wouldn't last very long in the Amazon Rain Forest unless you were in the company of an experienced guide or survival expert. So before we go stumbling into big trouble, let's get to know the terrain.

The Amazon Rain Forest covers about 40 percent of South America. It spreads across the Amazon Basin, the drainage system for the Amazon River. A drainage system is a land area that draws off floodwaters when a river rises. The Amazon Basin — also known as *Amazonia* — is the world's largest drainage system and covers an area of about 2.3 million square miles. Collectively, this river, basin, and rain forest are commonly called the Amazon.

Why is the Amazon Basin so immense? Because there's a *lot* of water to drain! Traveling west to east, the Amazon River is about 4,000 miles long — greater than the distance between San Francisco and New York City — and ranges from four to six miles wide. The river carries freshwater all the way from the Andes Mountains and northern Brazil to the Atlantic Ocean. The Amazon is second in length to the Nile River in Egypt, but it carries the largest water volume of any river on earth.

In 1541, the Spanish soldier and explorer Francisco de Orellana (c.1490–1546) led an expedition over the Andes Mountains. Orellana was helping Gonzalo Pizarro (c.1506–1548) search for the fabled "Land of Cinnamon," which was believed to be east of Quito, Ecuador. The mission proved disastrous. After many members of the expedition had either deserted or died, Orellana decided not to return over the Andes, and instead led his soldiers down the river until they reached the Atlantic Ocean.

Orellana was accompanied by the Spanish monk Gaspar de Carvajal (c.1500–1584), whose chronicles noted that the explorers were at one point attacked by female warriors. Carvajal described the women as very white and tall, with long, braided hair, and wielding bows and arrows. Some researchers believe that the expedition may have encountered the women of the Icamiabas tribe, and others suggest they may have misidentified grass-skirted male warriors. The attackers were likened to the Amazons, the female warriors of Greek mythology, and the river became known to Europeans as Rio Amazonas, the Amazon River.

More than 1,100 tributaries — smaller rivers and streams that lead into a larger river — flow into the Amazon. Seventeen of these tributaries are over 1,000 miles long. During the rainy season — April to August — 50 to 175 inches of rainfall causes some rivers to rise as much as thirty feet. That flooding leaves large areas of forest covered by water for up to eight months.

So what is a rain forest? By definition, it is a dense evergreen forest with an annual rainfall of at least one hundred inches. There are two types of rain forests: *temperate rain forests,* which are located near coastal areas, and *tropical rain forests*, which are close to the earth's equator. Most of the Amazon Basin is tropical rain forest — the Amazon Rain Forest — and the rest is savanna or scrubby woodland.

If you stand on the floor of the Amazon Rain Forest, under the thick foliage that makes up the *forest canopy*, you can look in any direction and see only the color green, which makes it pretty easy to lose your sense of direction. Thick, rope-like vines called *lianas* dangle down from the forest canopy, so if you were lost you might be tempted to climb up a vine to get a better view. Don't do it! If you pull on a vine, you're likely to pull down a large amount of *deadfall*, rotten timber that has become tangled among the higher branches.

Because the trees are so dense, much of the forest floor remains in shadow during the day. But you can't escape the heat. The temperature is 75 to 85 degrees Fahrenheit during the day and rarely dips below 65 degrees at night. Since the humidity is always high, the temperature feels much hotter. You can expect to sweat buckets!

Now you know that it's very easy to get lost in the Amazon, not to mention very wet. You'd better pack a compass, a rain poncho, waterproof hiking boots, and plenty of drinking water. Unless you replenish your body with freshwater, it will become dehydrated, losing water. You could also suffer heat stroke, where your body temperature rises dangerously high because you don't have enough water to cool your system. Both dehydration and heatstroke can kill people!

Since there's so much freshwater flowing through the Amazon, you might think that it would be easy to find drinking water. Think again! Just because it's "fresh" doesn't mean that it's free of parasites or diseases.

But parasites and diseases aren't the only things you might find in the waters of the Amazon. It is estimated that the rivers of the Amazon contain about 3,000 species of fish, including piranhas. Maybe you've seen adventure movies in which a school of hungry piranhas decides to eat some unlucky person for lunch? But it typically works the other way around, as many Amazon natives catch and eat piranhas!

There are at least twenty species of piranhas in the Amazon. It might surprise you to know that most piranhas are vegetarians, and none attack humans except by accident or in self-defense. Still, you probably shouldn't jump into a swimming hole without dangling some raw meat into it first. For all you know, the freshwater pool might be teeming with carnivorous red-bellied piranhas, which have interlocking, razor-sharp teeth. Sure, red-bellied pirhanas *might* leave you alone, but in the presence of an injured, bleeding animal, they have been known to eat their way down to the victim's bones within minutes!

A more dangerous fish is the electric eel, which generates an electric field around its body in order to sense prey. To stun or kill its prey, the electric eel will discharge 500 to 650 volts, five times the voltage of a household wall socket! Electric eels can grow several feet long; the larger the eel, the more powerful the shock.

Then there's the freshwater stingray, which is feared by many fishermen. Stingrays bury themselves in the sand or mud of shallow waters. If someone steps on them, they lash out with their tails, which are equipped with up to three venomous spikes. Although there haven't been any reports of people dying from a stingray attack, survivors say the "sting" is extremely painful.

You'll also want to watch out for reptiles in the waters of the Amazon. The anaconda is a giant snake, and can grow to thirty feet long and weigh over 400 pounds. Although anacondas are not venomous snakes, they do have sharp teeth and powerful jaws. They can remain underwater for ten minutes and are usually found at the water's edge, where they wait for prey. When an anaconda attacks, it typically coils around its prey and drags it underwater, but it can also use its muscular body to squeeze the life from an animal. This deadly squeezing ability is shared by the boa constrictor, a snake that is found in the trees and on the forest floor of the Amazon.

You should also be careful when admiring the poison dart frogs. These bright colored amphibians might look harmless enough, but even if you're really, really hungry, don't even think of nibbling on one! Their skin secretes a toxic mucus that can cause paralysis or death if it enters an animal's bloodstream. Why are they called poison *dart* frogs? Because some South American natives, such as the Chocó tribe in Colombia, treat the tips of their blowgun darts with this poison.

Even if you avoid all of these creatures, you won't be able to escape the mosquitoes. These insects can carry the dreaded disease *malaria*, which brings on fever, chills, and even death. Luckily, malaria can be treated, and the rain forest itself offers a remedy: quinine, which is extracted from the bark of the cinchona tree.

The Amazon Rain Forest is home to several million species of insects, plants, and animals, and most have yet to be identified. However, we do know the identity of the most harmful species in the Amazon: *humans.*

Industrial loggers, oil companies, ranchers, farmers, and land developers have already destroyed 13 to 16 percent of the Amazon Rain Forest. In 1995 alone, over 11,000 square miles of rain forest were destroyed in Brazil. After the trees are torn down, the land is often burned to kill off undesirable vegetation and animal "pests." What is the result of this? It is estimated that an average of 137 species are driven to extinction in the Amazon every day.

Burning the trees also pumps carbon dioxide into the earth's atmosphere, and it is widely believed that this causes increased temperatures through global warming.

Despite the increased awareness that rain forests

are an absolutely vital part of the earth's ecosystem, the Amazon Rain Forest continues to lose thousands of square miles every year. If this rapid rate of deforestation continues, many fear that much of the Amazon Rain Forest will be gone before the end of the twenty-first century. Instead of fearing the perils within rain forests, be more afraid of life *without* rain forests.

Antarctica

LOCATION: Wrapped around the earth's South Pole and surrounded by the Antarctic Ocean (also called the Southern Ocean).

DESCRIPTION: Covered under a massive sheet of ice, Antarctica is the coldest, windiest, driest, and highest continent on earth.

Even if you enjoy cold weather, you might think twice before you trek off to Antarctica. Why? Because unless you've been there, it's probably colder than you could ever imagine!

To get some idea of how cold Antarctica is, think about reaching into a freezer to get some ice cubes. Pretty chilly in there, right? The temperature inside the freezer has to be a minimum of 32 degrees Fahrenheit, because that's the temperature at which water turns to ice. But by Antarctica's standards, freezing temperatures are considered warm! Antarctica's average summer temperature is –4 degrees Fahrenheit, and its average winter temperature is –80 degrees.

And those are just the *average* temperatures in Antarctica! Yes, it can get warmer along the coast in the summer months, even up to 50 degrees. In winter, it can get a whole lot colder. Because of Antarctica's location at the "bottom" of our rotating world, it spends about half the year in sunlight and the other half in darkness. Sources vary, but some say that the Antarctic winter begins when the sun sets on March 21 and lasts until the sun rises again around September 23. During one winter, on July 21, 1983, the Soviet Union's scientific station *Vostok*, in the Australian Antarctic Territory, recorded the lowest temperature ever measured on earth: −128.6 degrees Fahrenheit.

But chattering teeth are the least of your problems. The cold can actually cause teeth to crack, and metal fillings to fall out!

The most life-threatening danger from the cold is *hypothermia*, the lowering of your body's core temperature. If your core temperature drops below 86 degrees Fahrenheit, you can lose consciousness. And if your core temperature drops below 78 degrees, you'll die. To prevent hypothermia, you should wear layers of protective clothing. Since you lose more body heat through your head than any other part of your body, always wear a hat!

During the summer months when the sun never sets, Antarctica is especially vulnerable to ultraviolet radiation. Because ice is highly reflective, goggles or sunglasses are necessary to protect your eyes from becoming *snow-blind*. Snow blindness is temporary, but it can be very painful and could prevent you from finding your way to the safety of a camp.

Exposed skin is susceptible to *frostbite*, which damages tissue by clotting your blood and forming ice in your cells. Frostbite sometimes results in the loss of fingers, ears, your nose, and other body

WHAT IS OPPOSITE ANTARCTICA?

Antarctica literally means "opposite the Arctic." After all, the Arctic Ocean is at the North Pole, and Antarctica is on the opposite side of the earth, at the South Pole. And as many geographers point out, the Arctic is a frozen ocean that is surrounded by continents, and Antarctica is just the opposite: a frozen continent that is surrounded by ocean!

But there's more to it than that. The word *arctic* is derived from the Greek word *arktos,* which means "bear." When the ancient Greeks looked up at the stars, they recognized stellar groups as *constellations,* imaginary pictures in the night sky. One such constellation was of a little bear, and one of its stars was the Pole Star, also called the North Star. Today, this constellation is known as the Little Dipper, and by its Latin name *Ursa Minor,* which means "little bear." Because of this bear constellation, the Greeks had an adjective to decribe the Northern Hemisphere: *Arktikos,* or "bearish." They referred to the Southern Hemisphere as *Antarktikos,* meaning "opposite the bear." It is from the word *Antarktikos* that we get the name *Antarctica.*

parts you wouldn't want to be without. At the average summer temperature of −4 degrees Fahrenheit, it takes a wind speed of only about nine miles per hour for exposed human flesh to begin freezing.

Speaking of winds, Antarctic winds can strike faster than you can run for cover, and quickly re-

In 1985, three scientists — Joseph Farman, Brian Gardiner, and Jonathan Shanklin — from the British Antarctic Survey reported a depletion in the *ozone layer* above Halley Bay, Antarctica. The area of depletion has become known as the *ozone hole*. Ozone is a form of oxygen, and it is most concentrated in the ozone layer of the stratosphere, at an altitude that ranges from nine to eighteen miles above the earth's surface. The ozone layer protects all living things by absorbing UV-B (a type of ultraviolet radiation) from the sun.

We need the ozone layer, because UV-B destroys microorganisms that are vital to the earth's ecosystem, and causes sunburn and skin cancer. Scientists discovered that man-made chemicals — particularly the refrigerant *chlorofluorocarbon* (CFC), which was widely used in refrigerators and air conditioners — had greatly contributed to the formation of the ozone hole. Fortunately, many countries listened to these scientists and have since strived to end the use of CFCs.

duce visibility to a few feet. The fierce coastal winds — known as katabatic winds — can exceed hurricane force (greater than 74 miles per hour) for several days at a time. In some areas, katabatic winds have been recorded at over 186 miles per hour!

How do these facts add up? Antarctica is the

coldest and windiest place on earth. And there is so little rain or snow that it is also considered the driest place — even drier than the Sahara Desert! Antarctica is actually an immense frozen desert, also called a *tundra*. But even though there's little snowfall, the winds can still whip up the existing snow into blinding snowstorms and make it impossible to cross the land.

But "land" isn't the right word. Why? Because about 98 percent of Antarctica's surface is completely covered by a massive sheet of ice. How big is this ice-sheet cover? About 5,274,126 square miles, or about the size of the forty-eight continental states and Mexico combined! In some areas, the ice sheet is miles thick. Cracks in the ice sheet form deadly crevasses, ice-walled fissures that can be thousands of feet deep. Some crevasse openings are only a few feet wide and are difficult to see during storms or because of the blinding sunlight.

The height of the ice sheet makes Antarctica the "highest" continent, with an average elevation of 7,500 feet above sea level. At the higher elevations, Antarctic explorers have suffered altitude sickness. In severe cases, altitude sickness can lead to *pulmonary edema*: Breathing becomes increasingly difficult and the lungs fill with fluid, which can lead to death. Because of the dry air, travelers must also drink plenty of water or risk becoming dehydrated.

In total, Antarctica has about seven million cubic miles of ice, or 90 percent of all the ice on earth. According to a popular estimate, if Antarctica's ice were to melt, it would cause global waters to rise about 200 feet. If that ever happened, coastal towns and cities would be submerged, and everyone in southern Florida would have to either relocate or learn to live underwater! Is there any need to worry? Not immediately — Antarctica has been buried under its ice sheet for over five million years.

The land on Antarctica that isn't covered by ice is mostly barren rock. Given the icy climate and terrain, very little can grow on Antarctica. In fact, it is the only continent without trees. So if you want to stay warm (and you will), don't bother to look for any firewood.

Without any trees, it's not surprising that Antarctica doesn't have any large land mammals or a native human population. However, Antarctica's shores and surrounding waters are abundant with wildlife, including blue whales, killer whales, several species of seals, Adélie penguins, emperor penguins, over forty kinds of flying birds, and about

200 different kinds of fish. It was primarily the hunt for whales and seals that attracted English and American explorers to Antarctic waters in the late eighteenth and early nineteenth centuries.

Who was the first person to set foot on the Antarctic continent? Historians are not sure. The ship log of American sealer Captain John Davis suggests that he may have sent a landing party to Hughes Bay on the Antarctic peninsula in 1821, but Henryk Johan Bull, a Norwegian who emigrated to Melbourne, Australia, definitely arrived on the mainland with six men on January 24, 1895.

In the early twentieth century, many explorers attempted to travel inland and be the first to reach the South Geographic Pole, also called the South Pole. In 1909, an expedition led by British explorer Ernest H. Shackleton (1874–1922) came within ninety-seven miles of the South Pole, but food shortages prevented them from reaching their destination. It was the Norwegian explorer Roald Amundsen (1872–1928) who first reached the South Pole, on December 14, 1911. Amundsen's team used special navigating equipment to calculate their position.

Unaware of Amundsen's accomplishment, British Captain Robert Falcon Scott (1868–1912) and four

This might sound confusing, but there are two South Poles! Not only that, there are two North Poles as well. How is this possible? Because the earth has a *geographic pole* and a *magnetic pole,* and the "ends" of these invisible poles terminate at different points.

To visualize the geographic pole, imagine a pole that runs straight through the earth, from the "top of the world" at the Arctic Ocean to the "bottom of the world" at Antarctica. This pole represents the earth's axis of rotation; the pole's "top" is the North Geographic Pole and the "bottom" is the South Geographic Pole. Globes of the earth are designed to spin on the geographic pole.

The magnetic poles are where the earth's magnetic field is most intense, and are located relatively close to the geographic poles. The South Magnetic Pole is in the Antarctic Ocean, and the North Magnetic Pole is near Greenland. Both magnetic poles may shift several miles during the course of a year.

companions arrived at the South Pole five weeks later, on January 17, 1912, where they found evidence that Amundsen had already been there. Scott and his team attempted to return to their base, but none of them survived.

Was Scott's expedition well prepared? Not by today's standards. One of their main problems was their thick, bulky clothing, which didn't allow their bodies to "breathe." When they perspired, their clothes became wet, and then both their skin and clothes began to freeze. Explorers and scientists have since learned that it's important for people to wear multiple layers of clothes in cold weather. Layered clothes trap air to provide insulation for the body, and can be removed or added to compensate for different temperatures and weather conditions. Today's explorers also have the advantage of special fabrics that prevent sweat from building up or spreading to outer layers of their clothes.

Even if you're wearing ideal clothing, keeping warm can be dangerous business. In 1934, the American admiral Richard Evelyn Byrd (1888–1957) suffered from carbon monoxide poisoning from a leak in his generator-powered stove. Expeditioners must be extremely careful when working with fire in huts or near tents, because the dry Antarctic air can cause a small fire to spread quickly. For this reason, open burning is now prohibited in Antarctica.

Even after all these years of exploration, getting to Antarctica is still difficult. The entire continent is completely surrounded by the world's stormiest seas: the merged waters of the southern Atlantic,

Pacific, and Indian oceans, which are together called the Antarctic Ocean or Southern Ocean. Antarctica is also surrounded by icebergs and *pack ice*, floating ice that is forced into a single mass. In winter, pack ice can extend out to 1,000 miles from the Antarctic coast, making the continent inaccessible to all ships except for heavily reinforced *icebreakers*, which can create their own path through the ice. All ships must take extra care along the shoreline, where gigantic masses of ice can break off from the coastal glaciers and crash into the water.

Airplanes fly to Antarctica during the summer months, but rarely risk the treacherous journey during the long winter. Round-the-clock darkness and the constant possibility of storms are only part of the problem. At temperatures below −58 degrees Fahrenheit, fuel turns to gel, which makes airplane flight virtually impossible. However, winter flights have been made in the event of emergencies. In 1999, a flight team rescued Dr. Jerri Nielsen, who was stationed in Antarctica when she discovered she had cancer; Nielsen was brought back to America, where she had surgery that saved her life.

Between 1957 and 1958, twelve countries participated in the International Geophysical Year, a program that encouraged and allowed scientists from all over the world to work together and share their research. These countries established over fifty scientific stations on the Antarctic continent and nearby islands. In 1959, representatives of the twelve countries signed the Antarctic Treaty, in which they agreed that no nation owned Antarctica. Furthermore, nuclear weapons would not be tested in Antarctica, and Antarctica would be used only for peaceful purposes such as scientific research. Today, Antarctica is home to over thirty year-round scientific research stations.

What do the scientists study? Geologists examine cross sections of ice, which can reveal the history of the earth's climates for the past 400,000 years, and may provide clues to future climate conditions. Roboticists have tested robots on the Antarctic ice in preparation for the robots to explore other planets and moons. In the summer, biologists study the wildlife on the coast. In the winter, astronomers take advantage of the months of darkness, observing the cosmos without being interrupted by daylight. Visibility is exceptionally good because Antarctica's air is very clean and free of dust.

However, the ultra-clean air can also be disorienting, especially in the summer months. If you go for a walk outside, you might think that nearby things are far away, and distant things may appear close. Why does this happen? Because the terrain is bright white, there isn't any haze, and there aren't any trees to gauge distance and elevation. The effect can be dangerous. An apparently distant crevasse might be right in front of you, or you might mistake a small box for a large building.

What's in store for Antarctica in the future? Since 1998, Antarctica has been officially designated as a global wilderness preserve. This means that no country can claim Antarctica as "private property," and every effort is made to preserve and protect Antarctica from any environmental damage. All the scientific stations are required to remove their waste and garbage, and cannot discharge sewage into Antarctic waters. Commercial exploitation is banned, as are mining and oil drilling, for a period of at least fifty years. Even sled dogs are banned, since dogs — on expeditions prior to 1998 — sometimes attacked and killed penguins and other native birds.

With its protected status, Antarctica could be preserved for many generations to come. Maybe you'll even wind up there one day. If you do, be sure to clean up after yourself, and bring a few extra pairs of socks, because one thing will definitely remain unchanged: Antarctica will still be *c-c-c-cold*!

Volcanoes of Hawaii

LOCATION: Hawaii, also called the Big Island, in the Pacific Ocean.

DESCRIPTION: An island made up of five volcanoes, one of which is considered the most active volcano on earth.

How would you like to have a volcano in your backyard? If you live on the island of Hawaii, you don't have much choice! That's because Hawaii is formed by five volcanic mountains: Kohala, Mauna Kea, Hualalai, Mauna Loa, and Kilauea. Together, they cover a lot of ground, about 4,028 square miles! Before we explore these volcanoes, let's find out more about volcanoes in general.

What is a volcano? To answer that question, we need to know that the earth is made of three layers: the *crust*, *mantle*, and *core*.

The crust makes up the earth's surface and is composed of rock. The crust is not a single, solid layer, but is made up of twelve massive plates. There are two types of crust/plates: *continental plates* (under the continents) and *oceanic plates* (under the oceans). The continental plates' average thickness is about nineteen miles, and the oceanic plates' average thickness is about three miles.

Below the crust is the mantle, a body of packed rock that is denser in composition than crustal rock. The mantle is about 1,800 miles thick and is neither solid nor liquid, but is more like hot asphalt. Because of this state, the earth's crust "floats" on the mantle.

Under the mantle is the core, which is made up of molten iron. The core is incredibly hot, with temperatures estimated at over 6,700 degrees Fahrenheit. This heat can melt rock from the mantle to create *magma*. Magma is molten, liquid rock that is less dense than solid rock and contains gas bubbles.

Heat and pressure make the magma rise up through the mantle, causing the earth's crust/plates to move apart. Rising magma can also force pieces of crust together, making them form mountains or underwater trenches. When the crust moves, it can be felt through earthquakes. Eventually, the magma may break through a *vent*, an opening in the earth's surface. This vent is called a *volcano*.

VOLCANOES FROM VULCAN!

The word *volcano* is derived from *Vulcan*, the Roman god of fire and craftsmanship. According to ancient myths, Vulcan lived below the surface of the island Hiera, one of seventeen volcanic islands that make up the Aeolian Islands (also known as the Lipari Islands) in the Tyrrhenian Sea, off the northeastern coast of Sicily. Eventually, the island Hiera became known as *Vulcano,* and similar geographic formations were called *volcanoes*. Scientists who study volcanoes are called *vulcanologists*.

Magma that reaches the earth's surface is called *lava*, and it can erupt from the vent with explosive force. When this happens, it can unleash *pyroclastic flows*, high-speed avalanches of hot ash and rock that can exceed 100 miles per hour as they move down the sides of the volcano. Pyroclastic flows can burn down anything in their path and cut down thick trees as if they were blades of grass.

However, volcanic eruptions don't always occur with massive explosions; lava has been known to bubble up and break through the earth's surface without a lot of noise. Either way, you'll want to steer clear of flowing lava, because it's still molten rock and very hot stuff. How hot? It depends on the lava's composition of minerals and gases, but some lava can be more than 2,000 degrees Fahrenheit and can set fire to nearly anything it touches.

Can you outrun flowing lava? If you're standing on fairly level ground, the answer is usually yes. The speed of flowing lava — called *lava flows* — depends on how much lava is coming out of the vent, and whether the lava is moving downhill. In many cases, people living near volcanoes have been evacuated before lava ever reaches their homes.

Although lava flows can destroy existing land and property, they can also create new land. How? Because lava eventually cools and becomes solid volcanic rock. Over many thousands of years, the lava can build up in multiple layers of volcanic rock and form a tall, sloping mountain called a *shield volcano*. All five volcanoes that make up Hawaii are shield volcanoes.

Eventually, magma can drain from underneath a volcanic mountain, and the mountain's top — the summit — will collapse, leaving a large crater in the mountain's summit. The volcanic crater is called a *caldera*, which is the Spanish word for cauldron.

Lava is not the only hazardous material to come out of volcanoes. Magma can heat underground streams and cause steam to explode out of volcanic fissures. Ash and cinders can be hurled miles into the sky, creating a particle haze that can block out sunlight and cause airplanes to malfunction. Lethal amounts of gases, such as sulfur dioxide and fluorine, can be discharged into the atmosphere.

But volcanoes also release things that help the earth, including two gases that are extremely important: hydrogen and carbon dioxide. The hydrogen mixes with oxygen and creates water vapor, and the carbon dioxide is crucial for plant growth.

Volcanic ash and dust also contain minerals that are beneficial to the soil, which explains Hawaii's lush forests.

Below its lush terrain, Hawaii also has thousands of earthquakes every year. The more powerful earthquakes can trigger landslides and large ocean waves called *tsunamis*. However, most of Hawaii's earthquakes are so small that you won't even notice them unless you're using a *seismograph,* an instrument that detects and records ground movement. The U.S. Geological Survey lists a total of eight destructive earthquakes that occurred on Hawaii between 1868 and 2001.

If the earthquakes seem scary, keep in mind that they are part of Hawaii's natural growth process. Below the earth's surface, magma (molten rock) rises up and pushes at earth's crust, shifting tectonic plates and causing earthquakes; the same rising magma may erupt through the surface and become lava, which is what "builds" Hawaii.

Would you be afraid of living so close to volcanoes? Over 143,000 people live on Hawaii, and it seems that most of them accept the volanoes as part of their lives. It's probably some relief that all the volcanoes are constantly monitored to anticipate any possible changes in their activity.

Scientists know of at least 1,500 volcanoes on earth and put volcanoes into three categories: active, dormant, and extinct. An *active volcano* is either erupting or has erupted in recent history and is expected to erupt again. A *dormant volcano* is inactive (not erupting) and may not have erupted for a long time, but it may erupt again. An *extinct volcano* is inactive and is not likely to erupt again, at least not for a long, long time.

Here's information about the five volcanic mountains that form Hawaii. We'll start with the oldest volcano and proceed to the youngest.

Kohala emerged above sea level over 500,000 years ago. It is estimated that Kohala's last eruption was about 120,000 years ago. Today it is considered an extinct volcano.

Mauna Kea rises 13,796 feet above sea level and is the tallest of Hawaii's volcanoes. If measured from the bottom of the ocean floor to the summit, Mauna Kea is the tallest mountain on earth! In Hawaiian, Mauna Kea means "white mountain," a name earned by its snow-covered upper slopes. It has not erupted in about 4,500 years and is now considered dormant.

Hualalai is the third youngest and third most active volcano on Hawaii. It had a lot of activity back in the eighteenth century, but has not erupted since 1800–1801. However, it is believed that magma rising under Hualalai caused a swarm of earthquakes that lasted over a month in 1929. Scientists predict this volcano may erupt again within one hundred years.

Mauna Loa is the second youngest and second most active. Its land area makes up about 50.5 percent of Hawaii. It is the largest volcano on the island, and is also the largest volcano on earth! In Hawaiian, Mauna Loa means "long mountain." It has erupted thirty-three times since 1843. At the time of this writing, it has not erupted since 1984.

Kilauea is the youngest and the most active volcano on Hawaii, and it emerged at sea level over 50,000 years ago. There have been thirty-four eruptions since 1952, and Kilauea has been erupting continuously since 1983! In 1975, a 7.2 magnitude earthquake beneath Kilauea triggered tsunamis that caused a lot of damage to the island's coast. In Hawaiian, Kilauea means "spewing" or "much spreading."

So now we know that Hualalai, Mauna Loa, and Kilauea are all considered active volcanoes. Of these three, which is the most dangerous? Any active volcano is dangerous, and it's difficult to determine whether one poses less of a threat than another. You have to consider not only the damage they've already done, but also the destruction they might cause in the future. For example, the lava flows from Hualalai's 1801 eruption have long since solidified, and now support Hilo Airport. If Hualalai erupts again, the airport could be in danger.

Historically, Kilauea is regarded as the deadliest volcano on Hawaii. In 1790, it produced a pyroclastic surge that killed many Hawaiian warriors and their families; historians disagree on the exact number, but most agree that at least eighty people perished. Since its 1983 eruption, Kilauea has spread lava over thirty-five square miles and destroyed over 180 homes. It has also created over 500 acres of new land and is probably still erupting as you read this very sentence! Some scientists have suggested that Kilauea may one day — thousands of years from now — cover all of Hawaii! In the twentieth century, Kilauea claimed at least four lives, which technically makes it "more deadly" than Mauna Loa and Hualalai during that same period.

But other scientists believe that Kilauea isn't nearly as dangerous as Mauna Loa, at least not for the short term. Why? Because Mauna Loa is so much larger, and an explosive eruption could go in many directions, producing lava flows far more destructive than those of Kilauea. According to the U.S. Gelogical Survey, it took about three years for Kilauea to spread lava over an area of about sixteen square miles, but Mauna Loa's 1984 eruption spread lava over the same amount of land in just three weeks!

It's also suspected that a buildup of magma under Mauna Loa created the greatest earthquake in Hawaii's recorded history: a magnitude 7.9 or 8 earthquake that occurred on April 2, 1868, and caused landslides and a tsunami that resulted in at least seventy-seven deaths.

Elsewhere on earth, volcanoes have caused even higher death tolls. In 1815, about 10,000 people were killed when the Tambora Volcano erupted on Sumbawa Island in Indonesia; the volcano blasted so much ash into the air that it destroyed crops, causing diseases and starvation that killed an additional 82,000 people. To date, this remains the worst volcano-related disaster in recorded history.

If you travel to Hawaii, you won't be alone. Kilauea is visited by about 2.5 million tourists every year, and many of them are dazzled by the volcano's beauty. Because a view of the flows is easily accessible by car, Kilauea has even been called the "drive-in" volcano. But don't get too comfortable at this particular drive-in. It's still a dangerous place!

Mount Everest

LOCATION: On the border of Nepal and Tibet, in the Himalaya mountain range.

DESCRIPTION: The highest mountain peak in the world.

If you've ever thought about taking up mountain climbing as a sport, you might have put Mount Everest on your "to do" list. Many climbers have been attracted to Mount Everest because it offers a unique challenge: Its summit is the highest place on earth.

And just how high is Everest's peak? Using Global Positioning System (GPS) equipment, a 1999 survey that was sponsored by the U.S. National Geographic Society determined that the height of Mount Everest is 29,035 feet. That's several feet higher than the previously estimated height of 29,028 feet, which had been established by the Indian government in the early 1950s, before the invention and development of GPS technology.

You can expect Mount Everest's height to change again, because it's actually growing! This is due to the shifting crustal plates beneath the Himalaya, the mountain range that includes Everest. According to one estimate, Everest's height increases by about 0.2 inches every year. At that rate, it will have grown a whole twelve inches by the year 2059!

For now, let's just say that the summit of Mount Everest is about 5.5 miles above sea level, higher than any other place on earth. It's a long way up and a long way down! It's also cold and windy. At the summit, the temperature never rises above freezing, and winds can exceed 177 miles per hour. Yikes!

Do you think "Everest" rhymes with "cleverest"? That's what just about everyone thinks, including mountain climbers and the people who write pronunciation keys for dictionaries. But according to historians, the correct pronunciation is EEV-rest. That's how it was pronounced by Sir George Everest, the British surveyor whose name was given to the mountain by the Royal Geographical Society in 1865.

Why was the mountain named after Sir George Everest? Because he had worked on the Great Trigonometrical Survey of India from 1818 to 1843, and helped to map the country with great accuracy. In recognition of Everest's accomplishments, his successor, Andrew Waugh, chose to name the mountain after "that illustrious master of accurate geographical research." Everest's achievements were indeed impressive, but it should be noted that he neither discovered nor ever saw the mountain that was named after him.

Between 1847 and 1849, three surveyors — all working on the Great Trigonometrical Survey of India — were in different locations when they each surveyed a tall Himalayan peak, which they respectively listed as "Peak Gamma," "Peak B," and "Peak H." By 1850, it was determined that peaks "Gamma," "B," and "H" were the same mountain, and it was renamed Peak XV. By 1856, Survey General Andrew Waugh concluded that Peak XV was probably "the highest in the whole world." Waugh claimed Peak XV was "without any local name that we can discover," and proposed it should be renamed in honor of the former Surveyor-General Sir George Everest.

Some historians maintain that the native Sherpas had long called the mountain Chomolungma, which translates as "divine wind mother" or "mother goddess of the earth." Others suggest that the name Chomolungma was applied to the Everest region, and not one particular peak. Either way, the Royal Geographical Society approved the name Mount Everest in 1865, but an increasing number of contemporary climbers — in respect to the Sherpas — call the mountain Chomolungma.

The Chinese call it Qomolangma Zang, a variation on the Sherpa name Chomolungma plus *zang* (mountain). The Nepalese call the mountain Sagarmatha, a combination of *sagar* (sky, heaven) and *matha* (head, top part).

What happened when the world first learned of Mount Everest's height? Not much. In the nineteenth century, *mountaineering* (mountain climb-

The Sherpas are an ethnic group who have lived in the Himalaya since the early 1400s, when they migrated from eastern Tibet (the word *Sherpa* translates as "Easterner"). For many centuries, Sherpas regarded the towering mountains as the homes of gods and goddesses, sacred places where they should not trespass. Their beliefs changed with the arrival of British mountaineers in the early twentieth century, and many Sherpas came to embrace mountain climbing as part of their own way of life. Sherpas have worked as guides or climbing partners on numerous expeditions and have summitted Chomolungma (Mount Everest) more times than Westerners.

ing) clubs existed in England and North America, but few climbers considered Mount Everest to be a realistic challenge. First of all, scientists knew that the air pressure became thinner at high altitudes, and that at altitudes less than three miles, balloonists and mountaineers could suffer from *hypoxia*, when the body doesn't get enough oxygen. Many people believed that the air atop Mount Everest was too thin to breathe.

Then there was the problem of getting to Mount Everest. It's between Tibet and Nepal, and completely landlocked, 700 miles away from the nearest seacoast in India. Bear in mind that the news of Everest's height came out before the invention and development of airplanes, so a mountaineer's journey to Everest would have taken several weeks!

Even if late-nineteenth-century mountaineers had been willing to make the rough trip, they would have encountered an even greater obstacle: Both Tibet and Nepal were *isolationist* countries, meaning they were closed to foreigners.

That situation changed in 1920, when the Tibetan government granted permission for a British expedition to explore Mount Everest. The English were especially keen on the idea of "conquering" Everest since they had failed to be the first to reach either the North or South Pole. At this point in history, *supplementary oxygen* (canisters or bottles filled with oxygen) had been used by aviators to prevent altitude sickness, but many mountaineers considered the devices — for their own sport — as "cheating." But mountaineers also acknowledged that Everest wasn't any ordinary mountain, as its summit is high above the elevation of 20,000 feet, the so-called death zone where oxygen is insufficient to sustain life for long periods.

In 1921, the Royal Geographical Society sent an exploratory expedition to find a route to the summit. English climber George Mallory reached a saddle-shaped piece of ground called the North

Col at an elevation of 23,000 feet, and believed he'd found a route, but high winds forced him to end his journey.

In 1922, a British expedition — using bottled oxygen — reached an altitude of 27,290 feet, but the effort to reach the summit ended when seven Sherpas were killed in an avalanche. The following year, an American reporter asked George Mallory why he wanted to climb the dangerous Everest, and Mallory replied, "Because it's there."

In 1924, Mallory climbed Everest with Andrew "Sandy" Irvine. They were last seen alive at an elevation of approximately 27,776 feet; they never returned, and Mallory's remains were not found until 1999. Did Mallory and Irvine perish before they could reach the summit, or had they reached the summit and failed in their descent? At the time of this writing, the answer remains a mystery. Climbers hope to discover the truth by finding the remains of Irvine, who carried a Kodak vest-pocket camera that could possibly yield photographic evidence of their climb.

There were more expeditions, and more failed efforts to reach Everest's summit. Then in 1950, Tibet fell under Chinese rule, and Mount Everest's northern and eastern slopes were closed off to climbers for the next thirty years. But that same year, Nepal opened its borders, which made Everest's southern slope accessible.

Finally on May 29, 1953, Tenzing Norgay (commonly identified as a Sherpa but born in Tibet) and New Zealander Edmund Hillary arrived at Everest's summit. Members of a British expedition, they had climbed to the top of Mount Everest and returned alive. Naturally, they became international heroes.

More expeditions followed, with climbers claiming various "first" records. In 1975, Junko Tabei of Japan became the first woman to climb Everest. In 1978, Reinhold Messner and Peter Habeler became the first team to summit Everest without supplementary oxygen. In 1979, Sherpa Ang Puh became the first person to summit Everest twice (but did not survive the second descent). In 1980, Reinhold Messner ascended again without oxygen, but this time he was all by himself, making him the first person to climb solo.

Over the years, climbers established at least thirteen different routes to Everest's summit. Many climbers agree that one of the most difficult routes is the Kangshung Face, which is on the mountain's east side. The most common route is up the south side, where climbers set up a series of camps so they can *acclimate* (adjust) to the increased elevations; if they don't acclimate, they will suffer from altitude sickness. Although some climbers choose not to use bottled oxygen, they must still take time to acclimate.

On May 10, 1996, Everest's summit was the destination for five different expeditions, two of which

THE HIGH COST OF CLIMBING

Is mountaineering experience the only thing you need to reach Everest's summit? Well, it helps if you have plenty of money. Travel expenses, climbing equipment, and other provisions can easily empty most wallets. The Nepalese government also charges a hefty "peak fee" to climb Everest. According to a 1996 report, the peak fee for one to seven climbers was $50,000 to $70,000, depending on their planned route, and there was a $10,000 charge for each additional team member up to a maximum total of twelve climbers. If the team decided to change its route, they were charged another $30,000. Expeditions were also charged a $4,000 garbage deposit.

The Nepalese government isn't the only one making money. Since the 1980s, commercial expeditions and professional guides have been paid to take climbers to Everest's summit for a fee, with prices typically starting at over $60,000 a person.

were commercial ventures: Mountain Madness of Seattle, and Adventure Consultants of New Zealand. The Mountain Madness expedition was headed by Scott Fischer, who had previously summitted Everest without supplemental oxygen. Adventure Consultants was headed by Rob Hall, an experienced guide who had previously summitted Everest four times, and had brought thirty-nine clients to Everest's summit. With so many successful expeditions, had climbing Everest become an easier task? In a 1996 interview, Hall stated, "With enough determination, any bloody idiot can get up this hill. The trick is to get back down alive."

As things turned out, Hall and Fischer didn't survive the journey. They were among eight climbers who died after an unexpected blizzard blasted Mount Everest with winds of over 70 miles per hour and subfreezing temperatures. Bad judgment had also played a role, as several climbers — including Hall and Fischer — had decided to continue their ascent after 2 P.M., which meant they wouldn't have enough daylight to return to their camp. This event gained an enormous amount of media attention and was the subject of several books, including *Into Thin Air* by journalist Jon Krakauer.

By the end of 1996, a total of ninety-eight climbers had reached Everest's summit, and fifteen climbers had died. A Dallas doctor named Beck Weathers — a member of Rob Hall's team — survived the blizzard of May 10, but not without injury; he lost his right hand, his left hand's thumb and fingers, and his nose from severe frostbite. In 1997, Weathers told a reporter for the *Providence Journal,* "The mountain grows exponentially more dangerous as you go up. If you have problems, it will occur in a way that leaves you significantly wounded. You never think it can happen to you."

Indeed, few people thought anything bad would happen to Babu Chiri Sherpa, one of Everest's most experienced climbers. He had summitted Everest ten times, twice within a two-week period in 1995. He held the record for the fastest ascent (sixteen hours fifty-six minutes) and longest stay on Everest's summit (twenty-one hours, and without bottled oxygen). But in April 2001, Babu Chiri was killed when he fell into a deep crevasse near his campsite at 20,336 feet. At the time of his death, Babu Chiri had been attempting his eleventh summit.

Since 1953, over 4,000 climbers have attempted to reach Everest's summit; over 1,300 climbers have succeeded, and over 170 have died in the effort.

As long as Everest remains open to climbers, it will attract people who are determined to make it to the top. The number of summitters will rise, and — unfortunately — so will the body count.

The Challenger Deep

LOCATION: 210 miles southwest of Guam, at the bottom of the Mariana Trench, a depression in the seafloor of the western Pacific Ocean.

DESCRIPTION: An underwater gorge, and the greatest ocean depth on earth.

Can you swim? If not, maybe you should learn. After all, about 71 percent of the earth's surface is covered by water! That means "dry land" only makes up about 29 percent of the surface of our planet, which could be called a "water world."

For most air-breathers, the ocean is a place of mystery. The average depth of the ocean floor lies 12,000 feet below sea level, or 2.3 miles down. But that's just the *average* depth, and the ocean floor — like the earth's land surface — has diverse terrain that includes mountains, valleys, and canyons. In other words, some areas are deeper than others. The deepest part of the ocean is estimated to be 36,198 feet below sea level, almost seven miles down. It's called the Challenger Deep.

The Challenger Deep rests in the Mariana Trench, an immense underwater depression that was first studied by the British scientific survey ship *Challenger* in the late nineteenth century. Although the trench is closer to Guam, it gets its name from the Mariana Islands to the north. The Challenger Deep gets its name from *Challenger II*, the British survey ship that located the deepest area of the Mariana Trench in 1951.

How was the Mariana Trench formed? If you read the chapter about Hawaiian volcanoes, you know that the earth's surface (or crust) is made up of twelve massive plates that "float" on the mantle, the molten rock of Earth's core. Essentially, the Mariana Trench is the result of a collision between the Philippine plate (a continental plate) and the Pacific plate (an oceanic plate); the collision forced the heavier Pacific plate down toward the mantle, and the edge of the Philippine plate was dragged down, creating a steep-walled trench.

So, how does the Mariana Trench compare with the Grand Canyon in Arizona? The Grand Canyon is 277 miles long, 18 miles wide, and nearly 1 mile deep. The Mariana Trench is 1,584 miles long, 44 miles wide, and over 4 miles deep (not including its depth below sea level).

And how does the depth of the Challenger Deep compare with the height of the earth's highest peak, Mount Everest? The Challenger Deep is at least 35,800 feet below sea level, and Mount Everest is 29,035 feet above sea level. That means the Challenger Deep is deeper than Mount Everest is high! If Mount Everest rose up from the bottom of the Challenger Deep, Mount Everest's peak would be over a mile underwater!

Since Mount Everest has lured so many mountaineers, you might think that the Challenger Deep has attracted many adventurous explorers. You'd be wrong! More than 1,300 climbers have summitted Mount Everest, but only two people have ever reached the Challenger Deep. That's fewer than the number of astronauts (twelve) who have walked on the moon!

Why have so few people visited the Challenger Deep? To put it simply, difficulty and danger. You probably knew this already, but humans can't breathe underwater without some sort of oxygen supply, or they'll drown (duh!). So if you're going to plan a trip to the Challenger Deep, you're going to need to bring your own oxygen.

Let's consider scuba gear. The word *scuba* is an acronym for Self-Contained Underwater Breathing Apparatus; scuba gear delivers compressed oxygen to your lungs and also *pressurizes* your body. Why does your body need to be pressurized? Well, when you dive underwater, the water's weight is pressing against your body from all sides. The deeper you dive, the more water surrounds you, and the greater the outside pressure on your body. This water pressure is called *hydrostatic pressure*. When you dive underwater, the pressure on the air in your lungs has to be the same as the hydrostatic (outside) pressure on your body. If your body is not properly pressurized (filled) with air, the pressure (weight) of all that water can crush your body! By using scuba gear, you breathe more oxygen than you do at sea level, and increase the air pressure in your lungs.

However, there's no way you can use scuba gear to reach the Challenger Deep. Most scuba gear is not designed for depths beyond 165 feet, where the hydrostatic pressure is about six times greater than it is at sea level, and a diver needs to breathe six times as much oxygen to stay alive. Since the hydrostatic pressure at Challenger Deep is estimated to be more than 16,000 pounds per square inch, you would be crushed flatter than a pair of ripe grapes long before you ever reached the bottom! Obviously, you are going to need something a bit more protective than a wet suit.

You'll also need some kind of heavy-duty lights and something to keep you warm. Even when the sun is shining over relatively clear waters, the sun's light and heat end far from the floor of the deep ocean. At about 650 feet below sea level, you'll be in total darkness, not to mention very cold.

How about a *submarine*, a ship that travels underwater? With its strong exterior hull and air-filled interior, a submarine allows its crew of *sub-*

mariners to explore the ocean without even getting wet! You could stay warm inside a submarine, and its lights would allow you to see in the dark depths. Unfortunately, great hydrostatic pressure can crush even the strongest hulls, and most modern submarines can't dive more than about 1,300 feet below sea level without being damaged by hydrostatic pressure. So a submarine might get you down to 1,300 feet, but you're still a long way off from the Challenger Deep.

Maybe you should try a *submersible*, a smaller submarine designed for greater depths and just a few passengers. These vehicles are also called deep-dive submersibles or deep submergence vessels (DSVs). Currently, there are only four submersibles that are rated (built and tested) to dive past 15,000 feet: The French *Nautile* and Russia's two MIR submersibles (*MIR I* and *MIR II*) are rated to 20,000 feet below sea level, and the Japanese *Shinkai 6500* is rated to 21,320 feet, or about four miles down.

Given that the ocean floor's average depth is 12,000 feet, any submersible that can reach 20,000 feet is capable of reaching 98 percent of the ocean floor. What about the remaining 2 percent, which includes the Challenger Deep? Sorry, but that's deeper than the ratings for any existing submersible.

So how *do* you get to the Challenger Deep? Didn't I mention that two people already went there? How did they do it? Their story begins, more or less, in the late 1940s, when Swiss physicist Auguste Piccard developed the first *bathyscaphe*. The word *bathyscaphe* (also spelled *bathyscaph*) is a combination of the Greek words *bathus* (deep) and *skaphe* (boat), and Piccard's invention was a maneuverable, free-diving, deep-sea research vessel. The bathyscaphe was a great advance from an earlier deep-sea vessel, the *bathysphere,* which was basically a steel sphere secured to a long cable that was winched (raised and lowered) by a support ship.

In 1958, the U.S. Navy purchased Piccard's third bathyscaphe, the *Trieste*. The *Trieste* was initially configured for depths of only 20,000 feet, but the navy made extensive modifications, including the installation of a new cabin: a spherical capsule that was six feet in diameter and weighed fourteen tons. According to the cabin's manufacturer, the cabin could endure pressures at 50,000 feet below sea level, if such a place existed! After the modifications, the navy began testing the *Trieste,* taking it out deeper and deeper in preparation for a journey to the ocean's greatest depths.

On January 23, 1960, Jacques Piccard (Auguste Piccard's son) and U.S. Navy Lieutenant Don Walsh took the *Trieste* down into the Challenger Deep. At about 6,000 feet, the chill prompted both men to put on warmer clothes. The descent lasted for four hours forty-eight minutes, and they felt a soft thump as they landed at the bottom, 35,800 feet below sea level.

Walsh and Piccard made observations and recorded data for about twenty minutes. Gazing through the *Trieste*'s single porthole, Piccard reported seeing a passing fish! This was quite a surprise, since many scientists didn't think any creature could live at the pressure of such depths. The *Trieste*'s return to the surface took three hours and seventeen minutes.

Although the Challenger Deep mission was a success, the navy subsequently restricted the *Trieste* to descents of 20,000 feet or less. In a 2000 interview for *Naval History* magazine, Don Walsh explained, "The navy felt the new cabin that was built for it was not safe and didn't want us to use it anymore." Walsh added, "If you can dive to 20,000 feet, you can cover 98 percent of the seafloor."

Before Auguste Piccard (1884–1962) developed the bathyscaphe, he designed the first airtight, pressurized gondola for high-altitude balloon flights. He and his twin brother, Jean-Felix (1884–1963), were famous for their balloon ascents. In 1931, Auguste and his assistant, Paul Kipfer, made the first balloon flight into the stratosphere, reaching a height of 51,777 feet.

Jean-Felix was instrumental in the development of a liquid oxygen converter and polyethylene high-altitude balloons, and set a U.S. record when he and his wife, Jeannette — the first licensed female balloonist in the world — reached a height of eleven miles in 1934. In 1963, Jean-Felix's son, Donald, and Ed Yost became the first people to cross the English Channel in a hot-air balloon.

Auguste Piccard's son, Jacques, joined his father on numerous dives in their bathyscaphes. (In 1960, Jacques Piccard and U.S. Navy Lieutenant Don Walsh became the only two people ever to descend to the bottom of the Challenger Deep, the deepest place on earth.) Jacques Piccard's son, Jacques, is also a record setter. In 1999, he and Brian Jones piloted their balloon, the *Breitling Orbiter 3*, on a twenty-day trip that took them from Switzerland to Egypt, but not by the direct route. In doing so, they became the first balloonists to make a nonstop balloon flight around the world!

The navy retired the *Trieste* in 1963 and replaced it with the *Trieste II*, which was retired in 1982. Today, both bathyscaphes sit in navy museums. No one has ever returned to the Challenger Deep. Many people consider the journey too dangerous, not to mention astronomically expensive.

10 feet:	Limit for most divers without oxygen supply, because pressure builds up painfully in the inner ear, sinuses, and lungs.
165 feet:	Limit for scuba divers.
1,300 feet:	Limit for most modern combat submarines.
2,000 feet:	Limit for the U.S. Navy's deep submergence rescue vehicle (DSRV) *Mystic*.
12,000 feet:	Average depth of the earth's oceans.
15,000 feet:	Limit for the U.S. submersible *Alvin*.
20,000 feet:	Limit for the French *Nautile* and Russian *MIR I* and *MIR II* submersibles.
21,320 feet:	Limit for the Japanese submersible *Shinkai 6500*.
35,800 feet:	The bathyscaphe *Trieste* arrived at this depth in the Challenger Deep.

According to Walsh, a manned return trip to the Challenger Deep could cost as much as $100 million dollars. But the Challenger Deep mission was hardly a loss, as it provided information and technology to prepare scientists for future deep-sea expeditions.

So, how much of the ocean floor remains unexplored? According to oceanographer Robert Ballard, if you were to put all of the deep-sea expeditions together, less than 1 percent of the seafloor has been investigated. In 1977, Ballard and J. Frederick

Grassle made one of the greatest scientific discoveries of the twentieth century from the submersible *Alvin* at the dark depth of 9,000 feet in the Pacific Ocean. There, Ballard and Grassle found animals living around the superheated seawater — measured at 650 degrees Fahrenheit — that came out of *hydrothermal vents* (areas where erupting lava replaces the seafloor between oceanic plates). This discovery shattered the scientific belief that life on earth depended upon *photosynthesis* (sunlight for support in the food chain), and proved that life could exist by the chemical reactions of a planet's energy, a process called *chemosynthesis*.

The discovery was not without risk. The hydrothermal vent-heated water melted *Alvin*'s temperature probe, which was made of the same material used for *Alvin*'s windows. You don't want your submersible's windows to melt at any depth, let alone 9,000 feet! Fortunately, only the temperature probe was damaged, but after that trip, heat sensors were added all around *Alvin*.

To decrease the risks of underwater exploration, scientists have developed unmanned robotic crafts that are equipped with various sensors and manipulators. These crafts are represented by two types: remotely operating vehicles (ROVs), which are remote-controlled by people, and autonomous untethered vehicles (AUVs), which operate on their own. One noteworthy ROV is the *Jason, Jr.*, used by Robert Ballard in 1986 to explore the sunken ship *Titanic*, which Ballard had located the previous year.

In 1995, Japan sent an ROV called *Kaikuto* into the Challenger Deep. *Kaikuto* recorded video images of a lugworm and several abyssal ghost shrimp at a depth of 35,788 feet, two feet shy of the *Trieste*'s record dive.

Scientists believe that ROVs and AUVs will continue to play a big part in deep-sea exploration. Don't be surprised if future expeditions take place on other worlds! Scientists believe that Europa, one of Jupiter's moons, is covered by a massive ice sheet that shields a thirty-three-mile-deep ocean. If there is water on Europa, there may be life, possibly thriving by chemosynthesis. NASA plans to send an unmanned probe, the *Europa Orbiter*, to investigate.

Meanwhile, unmanned probes will probably be the only visitors to the Challenger Deep. In that sense, the Challenger Deep is even less accessible to humans than outer space. After all, we only have to look up in the sky to see our moon, the sun, a few nearby planets, and billions of stars. For $20 million, you might even be able to hitch a ride with the Russian space agency up to the international space station. But could you buy a ride to the Challenger Deep for the same price? Probably not, because no one's heading that way!

Is there any reason for another human voyage to the Challenger Deep? Could we learn anything from it? Perhaps only that the journey is possible, but Jacques Piccard and Don Walsh already proved that over forty years ago.

So, I guess it's unlikely that you'll be going to the Challenger Deep anytime soon. Considering all the risks involved, maybe that's not a bad thing. But don't despair. There's still plenty of ocean to explore!

Tornado Alley

LOCATION: Central United States.

DESCRIPTION: A nickname for the area that is most frequently struck by tornadoes.

Maybe you've seen the movies *The Wizard of Oz* or *Twister*, but have you ever seen a real tornado? If you have, there's a good chance that you saw it in the United States, somewhere along Tornado Alley, because more tornadoes occur there than anywhere else on earth! Of the approximately 1,000 tornadoes that hit the United States each year, about 75 percent of them occur in Tornado Alley.

Where exactly is this place, and why does it get so many tornadoes? Don't worry, I'll tell you! I just don't want you to start packing a camcorder or a pair of ruby-red slippers until we go over a few tornado facts.

A tornado is a rotating column of air — a rapidly churning windstorm — that extends from a thunderstorm to the ground. The air column can rotate at speeds in excess of 300 miles per hour, which is far greater than hurricane force (over 74 miles per hour) and powerful enough to devastate anything in its path. Tornadoes can uproot trees, toss heavy trucks through the air, tear houses from their foundations, and transport objects over many miles. It is the most powerful storm on earth!

How do tornadoes form? Scientists aren't entirely certain, but they know that thunderstorms play a big part in making tornadoes. Actually, the word *tornado* comes from the Spanish *tronada* ("thunderstorm"), which may have been derived from the Latin *tornare* ("to make round by turning").

Do all thunderstorms produce tornadoes? No! The United States is struck by an average of 100,000 thunderstorms per year, but only about 1 percent (1,000) produce tornadoes. A thunderstorm that produces a tornado is called a *tornadic thunderstorm*.

Overland, most thunderstorms occur in the afternoon or early evening. Why? Because during the day, sunlight heats the air at the earth's surface, and this warm air begins to rise. You know that warm air rises and cold air sinks, right? That's because warm air is lighter and less dense than cold air.

Warm, moist air (water vapor) near the ground rises high up into the sky, where the water vapor becomes cooler, condenses, and forms a cloud. The top of the cloud may rise beyond the *troposphere*, the lowest level of the earth's atmosphere, six to ten miles above sea level, where temperatures are below freezing. Then the cold air begins to sink, but meets up with the rising warm air and begins to rotate and churn. You might think of this action as something like an invisible Ferris wheel: Warm air rises up from the ground, becomes cold air at the top of the "wheel" before it rotates downward, then meets with warm air and rises up again.

Within the cloud, small ice pellets — called *graupel* — may form and collide, producing electrical charges; positive-charged graupel rises to the top of the storm, and negative-charged graupel drops to the lower parts of the storm. The different charges result in a large, bright spark or electric burst called *lightning*, which can heat the air to temperatures as high as 54,000 degrees Fahrenheit. In case you're wondering, lightning is even hotter than molten lava (2,000 degrees Fahrenheit) or the surface of the sun (10,000 degrees)!

When lightning crackles across the sky, it literally burns through the air and creates a *vacuum*, an airless space. When the lightning's charge dies, the surrounding air comes rushing in to fill the vacuum, and it's this massive collision of air — *boom!* — that makes the sound of thunder. Since the speed of light is faster than the speed of sound, it makes sense that we see the lightning flash before we hear the thunder.

Okay, so now we have a thunderstom. What happens next? Well, here's what happens sometimes. Remember that "invisible Ferris wheel" of circulating warm and cold air? Imagine high, cold winds blowing at it and knocking it over sideways, but the "wheel" continues to rotate, something like the movement of an invisible merry-go-round in the sky. We now have a rotating thunderstorm, which is called a *supercell*. Not all thunderstorms become supercells, but supercells are credited with producing the most powerful tornadoes.

A supercell's area of rotation is called the *mesocyclone*, a radar term, and this rotation creates a powerful updraft. To be more precise, the mesocyclone is the supercell's rotating updraft, and it can be detected by radar. Since powerful tornadoes have been linked to supercells, meteorologists watch out for mesocyclones, as these suggest the possibility of *tornadic activity*.

WHAT IS RADAR?

The word *radar* comes from *radio detecting and ranging*. It is a method of using high-frequency radio waves to detect the size, location, and speed of distant objects that are on the ground, in the air, or underwater. The radio waves "bounce" off the surfaces of objects that enter or exist within a scanned area and create an image of the objects on a radar screen. Since its development in the 1930s, radar has been used extensively by military forces and weather services.

A mesocyclone may be two to six miles in diameter, and can be powerful enough to keep graupel (ice pellets) hovering within the cloud for many minutes. Graupel increases in size as water freezes to its surface, and when its size exceeds 0.2 inches, it is called *hail*. Not all supercells produce hail, but be aware that hail can "grow" to be larger than a baseball. Small bits of hail can cause serious injuries, and large hail can kill!

At the base of the thunderstorm, a cloud may appear to "drop" and bulge out from the upper layer of clouds. This lower cloud is called a *wall cloud*. Not all wall clouds rotate, but rotating wall clouds usually develop before tornadoes. With supercells, it's believed that *downdrafts* — arcs of sinking air — from the mesocyclone may play a part in tornado development.

If the wall cloud rotates, a *funnel cloud* (named for its shape) may form below it. A rotating funnel cloud often indicates the existence of a tornado. But remember, a tornado is defined as a rotating column of air that extends from a thunderstorm to the ground. If the rotating column of air does not reach the ground, meteorologists don't consider it to be a tornado.

Most tornadoes are *cyclonic tornadoes*, which

means that they rotate counterclockwise in the Northern Hemisphere (above the equator), and clockwise in the Southern Hemisphere (below the equator). Less common are *anticyclonic tornadoes*, which rotate clockwise in the Northern Hemisphere, and counterclockwise in the Southern Hemisphere.

If the U.S. National Weather Service (NWS) thinks a tornado is likely to form, it will issue a *tornado watch*. This means that weather conditions are "right" for a tornado, even though a tornado has not yet been sighted.

When a tornado is sighted, the NWS issues a *tornado warning*. If there's a tornado warning in your area, you should seek protective shelter in a

THE FIRST TORNADO FORECAST

Until the late 1940s, many people thought that tornadoes were unpredictible "acts of God." But in 1948, U.S. Air Force Captain Robert C. Miller and Major Ernest J. Fawbush analyzed weather data for a tornado that had occurred just five days earlier in Oklahoma, and they believed the evidence suggested they were in for a repeat performance. On March 25, 1948, they issued a warning, and they were right. A destructive tornado struck Oklahoma's Tinker Air Force Base a little after 6 P.M. on March 25, just as Miller and Fawbush had predicted.

basement, where you won't be exposed to wind and flying debris. Unfortunately, people confuse the terms *tornado watch* and *tornado warning*. It's important that you know the difference!

Tornado Watch = Watch out for possible tornadoes.

Tornado Warning = Find shelter immediately.

It's also unfortunate that some people are more determined to see a tornado than obey a tornado warning. According to the NWS, many tornado-related deaths and injuries are the result of people who ignore tornado warnings because they want to see the tornado.

Tornadoes come in many shapes and sizes. The funnel cloud may appear as a long, snakelike tendril called a *rope tornado*. It may also appear as a wide V-shape, known as a *wedge tornado*. Tornadoes may appear virtually transparent or very dark; their coloring comes from the dust and dirt that they draw up into the air.

A *waterspout* is a tornado that forms over water, but since it's not in direct contact with land, it isn't a true tornado. In fact, unless waterspouts hit land, they are rarely noted in tornado records.

Sometimes, a single thunderstorm may produce more than one tornado; these are called *multiple-*

When the U.S. National Weather Service sends out a *tornado warning*, it means a tornado has been sighted. Here's what to do if the tornado is in your area.

If you are in or near a house:

Go to a basement, storm cellar, or lowest level of a building. If there isn't a basement, go to a small inner room without windows, such as a bathroom or closet. Stay away from windows, since the tornado may blow in the windows and spray broken glass everywhere. If you can, get under a sturdy piece of furniture like a heavy table or workbench and hang on to it.

Don't waste time opening windows! You may have heard that unless a house's windows are opened before a tornado passes by, all the air will get sucked out of the house and it will explode. This is a total myth! A tornado can blast in windows whether they're open or closed, so opening them is a waste of time when you should be finding shelter!

If you are in a car or mobile home:

Get out and find shelter somewhere else! Do not try to drive away from a tornado because you might not be able to outrun it. *Do not hide under a highway overpass* because you might be struck by flying debris, or the tornado might level the overpass! If you're caught outdoors, try to find a ditch or gully and lie down in it, covering your head with your arms.

vortex (or *multivortex*) *tornadoes* or *tornado swarms*. In other cases, a small tornado may *orbit* (move around) a larger tornado; the smaller, orbiting vortex is called a *satellite tornado*.

As tornadoes move across the land, they may travel at speeds ranging from 5 to 30 miles per hour, but some have been clocked at over 70 miles per hour. They may last anywhere from several seconds to over an hour, but most last less than ten minutes. Don't let their size and distance fool you! Even brief tornadoes can be dangerous. They can increase speed and change direction, so if you see a tornado that appears to be far away, don't just stand around gawking or assume you can outrun it later! You should go immediately to a protected shelter or basement until the storm ends.

A tornado's traveling speed should not be confused with its circulating wind speed, which can be up to 318 miles per hour. Since scientists are rarely present when a tornado is occurring, how do they measure a tornado's wind speed? By examining the damage left in the tornado's path! Specifically, they examine damage to houses, vehicles, and trees. This method dates back to the early 1970s, when T. Theodore Fujita of the University of Chicago developed the Fujita Scale of Tornado Damage — also known as the F-scale — to measure a tornado's destructive power. The F-scale goes from F-0 to F-5. Here are the details:

The Fujita Scale (F-scale) of Tornado Damage

F-0: Gale tornado, 40 to 72 miles per hour. Can damage chimneys and break tree branches.

F-1: Moderate tornado, 73 to 112 miles per hour. Can peel shingles off roofs and push or overturn mobile homes from their foundations. The low end of an F-1 has the destructive power of a hurricane (*hurricane force* winds begin at 74 miles per hour).

F-2: Significant tornado, 113 to 157 miles per hour. Can tear roofs from frame houses, destroy mobile homes, and uproot large trees. Light-object "missiles" generated (in other words, the winds can send light objects shooting through the air like missiles). In some instances, investigators have found particles of straw embedded in trees, fence posts, and walls.

F-3: Severe tornado, 158 to 205 miles per hour. Can tear down roofs and walls on well-built houses, overturn trains, and uproot entire tree forests.

F-4: Devastating tornado, 207 to 260 miles per hour. Can level even well-constructed houses and blow buildings off weak foundations. Large missiles generated.

F-5: Incredible tornado, 261 to 318 miles per hour. Can tear well-built homes from their foundations, carry them into the air, and virtually disintegrate them. Can turn automobiles into missiles, launching them over distances of 327 feet. Bark is stripped from trees. Even steel-reinforced concrete structures are damaged.

Is there such a thing as an F-6 tornado? Only in theory. The F-scale actually goes all the way up to F-12, which equals Mach 1, the speed of sound (750 miles per hour), but scientists believe it is unlikely that tornadoes can achieve wind speeds above 318 miles per hour, in excess of an F-5. An F-6 is considered an "inconceivable tornado" because its destructive power is pretty hard to imagine. Think about it! If an F-5 can disintegrate well-built houses, how could an F-6 do worse? By disintegrating cars and trucks, too? Remember, the F-scale measures the damage caused by tornadoes;

if a tornado vaporized everything in its path, the F-scale wouldn't serve much purpose, because there'd be no damaged material to examine.

Fortunately, most tornadoes do not achieve wind speeds of 200 miles per hour, and only about 2 percent of all tornadoes are rated F-4 or F-5. Still, that counts for about twenty devastating or incredible tornadoes in the United States each year!

Now that we know a bit about tornadoes, it's time to visit Tornado Alley. You probably won't find it on most maps, because it isn't an official name; it's a nickname used by reporters, storm enthusiasts, and *meteorologists* (weather scientists). This is probably a big relief to real-estate agents, since they might have a tough time selling Tornado Alley property to people who suffer from *lilapsophobia*: the fear of tornadoes!

The American Meteorology Society places Tornado Alley in "the Plains area between the Rocky Mountains and Appalachians." According to a map produced by the National Oceanic and Atmospheric Administration (NOAA), Tornado Alley stretches down from southern South Dakota to northern Texas, covers most of Kansas, Nebraska, and Oklahoma, and includes eastern areas of Wyoming and

Colorado and western areas of Iowa, Missouri, and Arkansas.

What makes this large area so prone to tornadoes? Several factors. The Plains area is wide open, without tall mountains to inhibit winds. The Gulf of Mexico is to the south and sends moist winds over the region. The Rocky Mountains are to the west and send warm, dry air out over a higher altitude, about 3,000 feet. At about 10,000 feet, the *jet stream* — a high-speed wind — sends cool air flowing eastward at speeds that often exceed 250 miles per hour. All these layers of moist air, warm air, cool air, and shifting winds over flatland add up to ideal tornado-producing conditions.

How do the states in Tornado Alley rank for numbers of tornadoes? The National Severe Storms Center and Storm Prediction Center compiled the following Top Ten list:

Number of U.S. tornadoes between 1950 to 1994

(* indicates states within the area of Tornado Alley)

1. *Texas: 5,490
2. *Oklahoma: 2,300
3. *Kansas: 2,110

4. Florida: 2,009.
5. *Nebraska: 1,673
6. *Iowa: 1,374
7. *Missouri: 1,166
8. *South Dakota: 1,139
9. Illinois: 1,137
10. Colorado: 1,113

From this list, you can see that Tornado Alley isn't the only area that gets tornadoes. In fact, tornadoes can occur just about anywhere on earth and have been sighted in all fifty states! Again, keep in mind that few of these tornadoes ever reach F-4 or F-5 status.

Which state has had the most F-5s? According to one researcher, Kansas was struck by at least twelve F-5s between 1880 and 1989. What was the deadliest tornado on record? On March 18, 1925, a tornado killed 689 people as it traveled 219 miles across Missouri, Illinois, and Indiana. Although the F-scale hadn't been developed at the time, this "tri-state" tornado definitely left F-5 damage.

What was the biggest outbreak of tornadoes on record? It happened April 3–4, 1975, when 148 tornadoes touched down in thirteen states: Alabama, Georgia, Illinois, Indiana, Kentucky, Michigan, Mississippi, North Carolina, Ohio, South Carolina, Tennessee, Virginia, and West Virginia. This outbreak left 330 people dead and over 5,300 injured.

What city has been struck by the most tornadoes? Oklahoma City, with records of over one hundred tornadoes. On May 3, 1999, a swarm of over sixty tornadoes broke out over Oklahoma and southern Kansas, and the Oklahoma City metropolitan area was hit by its first F-5, which was a half mile wide and traveled thirty-eight miles in about thirty minutes. The combined tornadoes left forty-eight people dead, over 800 people injured, and a damage toll of over $1.5 billion. Fortunately, the National Weather Service had issued tornado warnings in advance of the storms, and many people survived because they had obeyed the tornado warnings and found shelter.

If you live in Tornado Alley or are planning a visit there, be sure to keep an eye on the sky and tune your radio for weather reports. If you hear a tornado warning, you know what to do!

Interstellar Space

LOCATION: Throughout the universe.

DESCRIPTION: The area between the stars, galaxies, and the sun and planets of our own solar system.

Have you ever thought about becoming an astronaut, floating weightless inside a spaceship or orbital station, far, far away from Earth? Maybe you've even imagined what it might be like to walk on another planet? You're not alone! Lots of people imagine the same thing, and many wonder why astronauts haven't traveled to other planets already. After all, astronauts have walked on the moon, and a six-wheeled data-gathering robot has rolled around on the planet Mars, so it shouldn't be too difficult to send humans to Mars, too, right?

Wrong. Any voyage through *interstellar space* — the space between the stars and planets — is a dangerous undertaking. The longer the mission, the greater the risk. A round-trip from the earth to the moon has been done within eight days, but a one-way trip to Mars takes several months. Sure, astronauts might survive the long journey to Mars, but it's a lot easier to send robots.

What makes space travel so difficult for humans? Plenty! Interstellar space is a *vacuum*, which means it's an airless environment; without any oxygen, space doesn't have a breathable atmosphere, or ozone to protect you from harmful radiation. If you're going to travel through space, you'll need a *spacecraft*, a vehicle designed to fly beyond Earth's atmosphere. Besides protecting you from radiation, the spacecraft must have an oxygen system and contain all the food and supplies you'll need to carry out your mission.

When your spacecraft is in a vacuum, you can't open a window to get a breath of fresh air, so the spacecraft's oxygen system is vitally important. However, oxygen itself has its dangers. On January 27, 1967, American astronauts Virgil I. "Gus" Grissom, Edward H. White II, and Roger B. Chaffee died within an *Apollo* space capsule during a simulated countdown, a month before their scheduled spaceflight. What went wrong? Until this accident occurred, NASA filled space capsules with 100 percent pure oxygen, which is highly flammable. An investigation revealed that a small spark within the capsule probably ignited the fire, setting some fabric ablaze and filling the *Apollo* capsule's airtight interior with smoke. It was not the physical contact with fire that killed the three astronauts but the smoke and sudden loss of oxygen. After this incident, NASA began mixing oxygen with other gases to reduce the risk of fire.

Airless space begins about seventy-five miles away from Earth, and it takes about twenty-five additional miles for your spacecraft to achieve *orbit*, a point where your spacecraft can revolve around Earth. How will you and your spacecraft get there? Unless your spacecraft is capable of launching itself directly into space, you'll need a *launch vehicle*. The standard launch vehicle is a projectile called a *rocket*.

A rocket contains fast-burning fuel, which can be in either solid or liquid form. Rocket fuel is *combustible*, which means it burns. The burning fuel produces a reaction of gases that propels the rocket. Unlike jet engines, which require an air-filled environment to operate, rockets contain their own internal supply of oxygen and can operate in a vacuum. Therefore, a rocket is an *internal combustion engine*, and its contents are highly explosive.

So be warned: Rockets should be handled with care! Accidental explosions were especially frequent during the early years of the "Space Race," when the United States and the Soviet Union (now Russia) used space exploration as a competition to prove technological superiority, and tested many experimental rockets. One of the most disastrous rocket accidents occurred in October 1960 in Tyuratam, in the Soviet republic of Kazakhstan, when a bad wiring connection triggered the explosion of an unmanned Soviet two-stage rocket. The rocket blew up on its launchpad during a test and killed at least ninety-two people.

Everything bound for space — astronauts, supplies, satellites, and spacecraft — is referred to as the rocket's *payload*. If the payload is more than one rocket can carry, multiple rockets will deliver the payload in installments. This method is being used for the construction of the International Space Station, which was designed with interlocking *modules*, self-contained units for specific tasks, such as living quarters and laboratories. Each module is constructed on Earth and launched into space, where they are assembled in orbit.

To leave a planet, a rocket must be able to achieve *escape velocity*, a speed that varies depending on the planet's gravitational pull; to leave Earth, escape velocity is a speed of 25,000 miles per hour, or about 7 miles per second. A rocket has to burn a large amount of fuel to reach that speed, and all that fuel, along with the payload, increases the rocket's weight. Instead of using a single rocket with a massive fuel tank to deliver the payload to space, scientists have developed economical alternatives: *multistage rockets* and *booster rockets*.

A multistage rocket might look like a large sin-

Three scientists are considered to be the founding fathers of rocketry: Russian Konstantin Tsiolkovsky (1857–1935), American Robert H. Goddard (1882–1945), and German Hermann Oberth (1894–1989). Working independently, all three scientists believed that liquid-fueled multistage rockets could be developed for space travel. Goddard fired the first liquid-fuel rocket on March 16, 1926.

One of Oberth's assistants was Wernher von Braun (1912–1977). Together, they worked on the devastating V1 and V2 rockets for the German Army during World War II. After the war ended in 1945, they came to America. Eventually hired by NASA, von Braun invented the *Saturn* rocket that sent the *Apollo* spacecraft to the moon.

gle rocket, but it is actually made up of two or more rockets that are "stacked" on top of each other. The stacked rockets fire in successive stages, one after the other, in a series of controlled explosions; when each stage uses up its fuel, it falls away from the rocket, and the next stage fires to continue the rocket's ascent and carry the payload higher. This method is used to launch satellites and manned space capsules.

Booster rockets are used in combination with a spacecraft's rocket engines, and literally give spacecraft a big boost up through Earth's atmosphere. To aid in liftoff, the space shuttle employs two solid-fuel booster rockets (called solid rocket boosters, or SLBs), which are jettisoned two minutes after the shuttle's launch.

But booster rockets are no less dangerous than any other rocket. A tragic launch accident occurred on January 28, 1986, when the American space shuttle *Challenger* lifted off from Kennedy Space Center in Florida, carrying Gregory B. Jarvis, Sharon Christa McAuliffe, Ronald E. McNair, Ellison S. Onizuka, Judith A. Resnik, Francis R. "Dick" Scobee, and Michael J. Smith. Seventy-three seconds after liftoff, *Challenger* suddenly exploded,

AN ALTERNATIVE TO ROCKETS?

For years, scientists and engineers have been working on the development of reusable launch vehicles (RLVs). Unlike reusable space shuttles that require expendable booster rockets to reach space, or space capsules that have to return to Earth by parachute, RLVs will be able to lift off from Earth, enter space, and fly back to Earth without casting off any expendable parts.

If you're waiting for an RLV to ferry passengers into space, you'll have to wait a bit longer. In 2001, NASA stopped development of the X-33 RLV, which had been conceived as a replacement for the space shuttle. Until RLVs are produced, the use of rockets and space shuttles will continue.

scattering debris high over the Atlantic Ocean. The entire crew was killed. What went wrong? Investigators found fault with one of the right booster rocket's O-rings, thirty-seven-foot-diameter rubber rings used to seal the rockets and prevent hot gases — by-products from the burning fuel — from leaking out. Cold weather had affected the O-ring, making it unable to seal properly. After the rockets fired, hot gases ruptured the O-ring, allowing liquid oxygen and hydrogen to mix prematurely, causing the right booster rocket to explode.

Okay, so now you know that getting to space isn't easy. But let's say that your launch has gone well, your spacecraft has entered space, and you're now free of the effects of Earth's gravity. That's right, you're floating within the spacecraft, feeling light as a feather, and doing midair somersaults with ease! This is all pretty fun, but weightlessness, or zero-g (the g is for gravity), does have some disadvantages.

For example, let's say all those somersaults make you so dizzy that you feel sick to your stomach. Since there isn't any "up" or "down" in interstellar space, you can't literally "throw up," but you can still "throw out." And unless you can contain that mess fast, it will float around the inside of the spacecraft and might clog delicate instruments. Yuck!

Even if you don't get ill, weightlessness will take its toll on your body in other ways. All astronauts have experienced *orthostatic collapse*, or "lazy heart," because the heart loses its normal tone when it is pumping weightless blood. *Osteoporosis*,

WHO WAS THE FIRST HUMAN IN SPACE?

On April 12, 1961, Russian cosmonaut Yury Alekseyevich Gagarin (1934–1968) blasted off from the Baikonur Cosmodrome in the spacecraft *Vostok I*. During his 108-minute flight, he traveled at a speed of 16,988 miles per hour, at an altitude that ranged from 112 to 203 miles, and completed one orbit around the earth. Proclaimed to be the first human to reach space, Gagarin became an international hero.

But was Gagarin really the first? Some historians aren't so certain. In 1961, Dennis Ogden, the Moscow correspondent for the British communist newspaper *The Daily Worker*, reported that another cosmonaut, Sergey Vladimirovich Ilyushin, had made an orbital flight just a few days before Gagarin. This event was the subject of the documentary film *Cosmonaut Cover-up*, which presented evidence that Ilyushin had lost consciousness during his flight and crash-landed in China, where he was detained (and later released) by the Chinese. Allegedly, the Soviet Union concealed this information because it did not want to admit any errors with its space program.

a softening of the bones, is also caused by weight-lessness. During long periods in zero-g, astronauts must exercise more than usual to maintain strong bones and muscles, but exercise alone can't prevent these effects.

Sometimes you might forget that you're weight-less, and this could lead to trouble. You'd better not be daydreaming about being on Earth when one of your fellow astronauts asks, "Could you please hand me that wrench?" Just hand it over slowly, and don't toss it! Even though the wrench — like everything else in the ship — is weightless, it still retains *mass*, which is the measure of an object's resistance to acceleration. If you throw the wrench within the spacecraft, there isn't any gravity to slow its speed and cause it to fall to the floor; instead, the wrench will become something like a launched missile. Trust me, the wrench won't feel "weightless" when it strikes your fellow astronaut with great force! To prevent this sort of an accident, astronauts make slow, careful movements inside their spacecraft, and use magnetic tools that can be easily secured to walls.

Now that you're in space, how about a trip to a space station? A space station is a manned satellite that orbits Earth and has one or more docking ports for spacecraft. Space stations are used for scientific experiments and astronomical observations, and may one day be used as a site for assembling spacecraft bound for other planets. If the space station is substantially larger than your spacecraft, you can also use it as a place to stretch your legs.

When you're on a spacecraft or a space station, you'll be exposed to many life-threatening dangers

THE MIR SPACE STATION

In 1997, the Russian space station *Mir* (Russian for "peace") was the site of a series of accidents and technical problems. In February, an oxygen-generating canister caught on fire. In June, a *Progress* cargo rocket rammed *Mir*, puncturing the laboratory module and causing *depressurization*, or loss of air. On two different occasions, computer failures set the station adrift. Fortunately, no cosmonauts or astronauts were injured in these mishaps.

Despite these accidents, Russians continued to regard *Mir* with great pride, and with good reason. Over one hundred cosmonauts and visiting astronauts used *Mir* between 1986 and 1999. In comparison, the U.S. space station *Skylab* was used by nine astronauts over a nine-month period between 1973 and 1974 (in 1979, *Skylab* fell out of orbit and sent debris over the Indian Ocean and Australia). Russia eventually abandoned *Mir* to concentrate on the International Space Station. In 2001, after fifteen years in space, *Mir* was guided by remote control to crash into the Pacific Ocean.

from space itself. What will you do if a blast of solar radiation knocks out your electrical equipment, or if your vessel is struck by a meteoroid or a piece of space junk from some previous mission? Obviously, you don't want any accidents to happen in space. When you're over a hundred miles away from Earth, it's not like you can just call the electric company or the National Guard and ask them to send someone over!

Who can you call? If you're lucky, you'll have a highly skilled ground crew, people who remain on Earth and maintain radio contact with your ship to help your mission. In April 1970, the spacecraft *Apollo 13* was on its way to the moon, about 200,000 miles from Earth, when the command module's oxygen tank exploded. Astronauts James Lovell, John L. Swigart, Jr., and Fred W. Haise, Jr., had to scrap their lunar mission and use their lunar module as a lifeboat. They also had to figure out a way to return to Earth! Fortunately, they were aided by Mission Control in Houston, and they made it back alive.

Reentering Earth's atmosphere (this is called *reentry*) is also hazardous. When a returning spacecraft hits the atmosphere, air friction can heat the vessel's exterior as high as 3,000 degrees Fahrenheit, which is more than enough to melt steel. Even if you have special thermal barriers to protect you from the intense heat, a lot can go wrong between reentry and a perfect landing. In 1967, Russian cosmonaut Vladimir Komarov had made seventeen orbits around Earth before reentry, but his *Soyuz 1* capsule's parachute snarled at 23,000 feet and the capsule crashed at 200 miles per hour. In 1971, cosmonauts Georgy T. Dobrovolsky, Vladislav N. Volkov, and Viktor I. Patsayev were returning from the first Soviet space station, *Salyut 1*, when their spacecraft, *Soyuz 11*, lost air during reentry, killing all three cosmonauts.

Now that you know the risks of leaving Earth, living in space, and reentry, let's consider a trip to Mars. The distance between Earth and Mars varies as both planets rotate around the sun. Mars is closest to Earth when both planets are in *opposition*, lined up on the same side of the sun. When Mars is closest, it's within 37 million miles; when Mars is farthest from Earth, it's 248 million miles away. That's a big difference! If we're going to travel to Mars, it makes sense to plan the trip when Earth and Mars are in opposition, which occurs once every two Earth years. By taking advantage of the opposition, we'll be conserving fuel and all the supplies we'll need to survive.

Even if we travel during the Earth/Mars opposition, the journey to Mars will take about seven months. Can humans survive in weightlessness for that long? Yes, at least in Earth orbit. Between 1994 and 1995, cosmonaut Valery Polyakov set the record for the longest stay in space — 438 days! — on the *Mir* space station. But not everyone is so well-suited for a long-term mission. In 1987, cosmonaut Alexander Laveikin had been on *Mir* for six months when he began registering an abnormal heartbeat. Doctors in the Soviet Union ordered Laveikin to return to Earth, which he did.

How long would we stay on Mars? Probably over a year, if only so we can take advantage of the next Earth/Mars opposition to return to Earth. Including the travel time, a mission to Mars could mean that we're away from Earth for three years or more.

Three years. Just think of all the oxygen, water, and food you would need for the trip. Do you see why it's easier to send robots? Except for their batteries, they don't require nourishment. They're ideal long-distance travelers. They never argue or complain, never get ill or bored, and never feel lonely or homesick.

But here's the greatest difference between robot and human explorers: Humans *want* to go to Mars. Is the human desire to go to Mars reason enough to make the trip? Certainly, the trip will bring us incredible experience and knowledge and open up whole new areas for scientific study. But before we go blasting off to Mars just because it's there, let's consider the fate of several unmanned spacecraft.

Mars 6 (Soviet Union, 1974): During its landing, the descent module transmitted data from the Martian atmosphere. Unfortunately, the data was unreadable due to a flawed computer chip, and contact was lost when the lander hit the planet's surface.

Viking 1 and *Viking 2 orbiters and landers* (U.S., 1975): Successfully landed and transmitted an enormous amount of data back to Earth.

Mars Observer (U.S., 1992): Lost communications after entering the Martian atmosphere.

Mars '96 Orbiter (Russia, 1996): Failed during liftoff from Earth and was destroyed.

Pathfinder (U.S., 1997): Successfully landed and deployed the six-wheeled robot named *Sojourner*.

Mars Climate Observer (U.S., 1998): Burned up in the Martian atmosphere.

Nozomi (Japan, 1998): Originally scheduled to reach Mars in 1999, but a course correction forced it to expend propellant; on its present course, it won't reach Mars before December 2003. Estimated cost: $848 million.

Mars Polar Lander (U.S., 1999): Lost communications. Estimated cost: $327.6 million.

Deep Space 2 (U.S., 1999): Was attached to the *Mars Polar Lander* (above). Estimated cost: $29.2 million.

Despite the few successful missions, the accidents and failures aren't exactly encouraging for a human expedition. Neither is the fact that no spacecraft or robot has ever returned from Mars. Granted, for all of these missions, the goal was to reach Mars, not return from it. Currently, there are plans to send robots to Mars and have them collect and deposit rock samples into a rocket that will be launched into Martian orbit, where a robotic space-craft will retrieve the samples and deliver them to Earth. It's conceivable that a human expedition might return in a similar fashion.

If we want to get to Mars, we have our work cut out for us. And space will remain an extremely dangerous place.

Ryder Windham was born in Watertown, New York, on June 19, 1964, the same day that the U.S. Senate passed the Civil Rights bill, and the Beatles released their recording of "Long Tall Sally." Since third grade, he has been able to recite the alphabet backward faster than he can say it forward. Whenever he eats pumpernickel bread or raw carrots, he hiccoughs. He has written numerous *Star Wars* children's books and comic book scripts, and collaborated with artist Kilian Plunkett on the comic series *Trouble Magnet: The Adventures of Witlock the Robot.* He doesn't think there's anything wrong with keeping a dictionary next to your bed in case you need to look up words in the middle of the night. He lives with his family in Providence, Rhode Island.